PAPAO

Management Model

Organize Large Initiatives

Kasper Dannefer

With

Troels Jakobsen, CaSandra Minichiello & Dale Ray Thiesen

Published by: Lean Agile Ltd
1st edition

Foreword

By Troels Jakobsen

Kasper and I have often discussed selections of frameworks and try to explain to our students that agile might not always be the correct approach. We come from very different backgrounds, but we have reached similar conclusions. This work is a discussion around the selection of framework and project models. The discussion around selecting frameworks is the evaluation of how agile we can be and how much structure and control we can expect. Demanding control in ever-changing environments is like asking raindrops to stop falling. As much as we want to control it, things just go differently. We are asking for flexibility, predictability and control all at the same time. Problem is that you can't have all. Somethings need to give. It is this discussion Kasper has leaped into with this work. Enjoy this deep dive into the project space of developing, managing, and supporting deliveries.

Introduction

When you as a manager, project manager, leader, or subject matter expert and are handed a large initiative, you need to ask yourself these two questions:

1. What is the initiative's lifespan; Is it short-lived or continuous?
2. Do we have previous experience in solving challenges like this, or is this a new area for us?

These two questions might be the information you need to determine the proper framework for solving the upcoming work.

In today's corporate world, many large initiatives automatically call for the assignment of a project manager. Often this project manager comes from the project management office (PMO), or a project manager is found internal or external to the organization. It is often up to the project to define what happens when the work is delivered. Projects risk ending up drifting into never-ending support or continuously add new development. Yet, there's a demand from corporate to follow the project methodology adopted in the organization. This well-defined methodology toolkit is perceived to solve anything thrown at it. To broaden the horizon, ask what framework will be best suited to solve the work at hand.

Nowadays, any organizational change seems to be towards an agile transformation. But often, it turns out that the organization has a lot of previous experience in solving the challenges that lie ahead. It can be in the form of known processes or the ability to hand over the business or customer's solution. Yet the new black is agile organizations. Agile is perceived as the fix for anything. However, they forget that the most change in agile lies with management. And the change ends up not solving the problems.

Asking the above two questions can pinpoint what methodologies could be the best to solve the challenges that lie ahead. In this book, we explore the simplicity of four methodologies. We try <u>not</u> to bend them into unneeded problem solving but use them for what they are best used.

This book will explore in the following order:

- ❑ Projects
- ❑ Agile Projects
- ❑ Agile
- ❑ Operation

To answer the above two questions, we end up with an intriguingly simple quadrant for selecting the suitable methodology, which in the last chapter will reveal the philosophy of the

- ❑ PAPAO Management Model

What to expect

This book is not trying to give a thorough description of how to use each method. The overview of each management area is a high-level description. It is meant as a what and a why, not a how. The purpose is to give enough background to put the above two questions into perspective.

Table of Contents

1. *Traditional Project Management* 1
   Waterfall method 4
   Suitability 6
2. *Agile Project Management* 9
   Core Functions of modern project management 11
   Integrated Project Functions (External Influence) 12
   Overarching Administrative Functions 14
   Suitability 15
3. *Agile Development* 17
   Why the "Agile Manifesto"? 21
   Agile Frameworks 25
   Agile Transformation 27
   Mixed Models 28
   Suitability 31
4. *Lean Operation* 35
   Origins of Lean 37
   Five Principles of Lean 38
   Lean Toolbox 41
   Where to Begin 43
   Lean Management 44
   Project Charter 46
   DMAIC 47
   Factors that Impact Application 49
   Leaders of Lean 52
   Project Closure 54
   Suitability 55

5. ***PAPAO management model*** *57*

Lifespan 57

Experience 61

The quadrant 63

Interoperability 65

Fit for Frameworks 71

Conclusion 76

1. Traditional Project Management

Let's put traditional project management into the proper context before we get into describing it. This method is also known as phase gated project management or waterfall project management. One phase needs to be completed before the next one is started. This method was born long before computers and software. The projects that were completed using these methods were the massive construction projects of things like the Egyptian Pyramids and Roman Colosseum. These construction projects had activities that had to be achieved using a structured sequence of steps. The requirements to complete each step of the work were decided in advance, and it was important not to change the plan partway into the project. The techniques used are still universally accepted and understood even though adaptability is now the more accepted method.

The construction industry is a bastion for traditional methods of project management. It stands to reason that when building an office building, a bridge, or the home you're going to live in, things must be done in the correct sequence. This is so that you don't do work that has to be undone later. The roof doesn't go in before the foundation. The concrete foundation is not laid until all the pipes that provide water are laid. The same goes for running electrical installations in the structure walls; Putting up the wallboard before that happens leaves much work to undo before completing the job. A disciplined, linear, step-by-step project management method is still the best approach for construction achievements.

The traditional way is where cost, schedule, performance, and risk are controlled. Traditionally managed projects follow the same five stages of *initiating, planning, executing, controlling*, and *closing* every time.

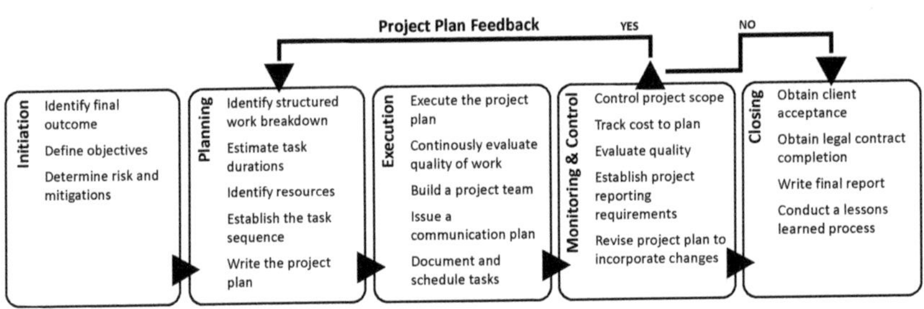

Gantt charts are a technique used in traditional project management to visualize this flow. Gantt charts provide a valuable visual reference for an overview of the project's status. Its most useful information is the timeline indicating progress on tasks. Many software tools offer ways to simplify creating the charts, but it can also be done on a standard spreadsheet.

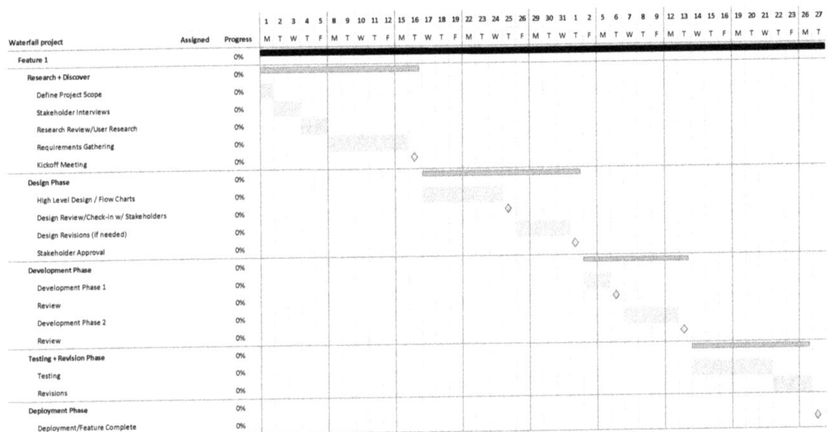

The essential information is the task description, start and end date. Also, take notice of the sequential nature of the tasks. A task must finish before the next task begins. That is a typical traditional project management concept. Gantt charts are an organizational tool for the project manager to show stakeholders the project's status at a single glance. For complex projects with hundreds, if not thousands of tasks, a Gantt chart's usefulness can be marginalized. For that reason, compartmentalizing a family of Gantt charts across a project is a more effective way to maintain Gantt's value to show project status for a smaller set of tasks.

The three project constraints that get the most attention are cost, schedule, and performance. They are universal to all projects, and it is the project manager's task to keep these within planned parameters. Traditional project management methods are unforgiving, graphically showing project management's failure to meet these constraints.

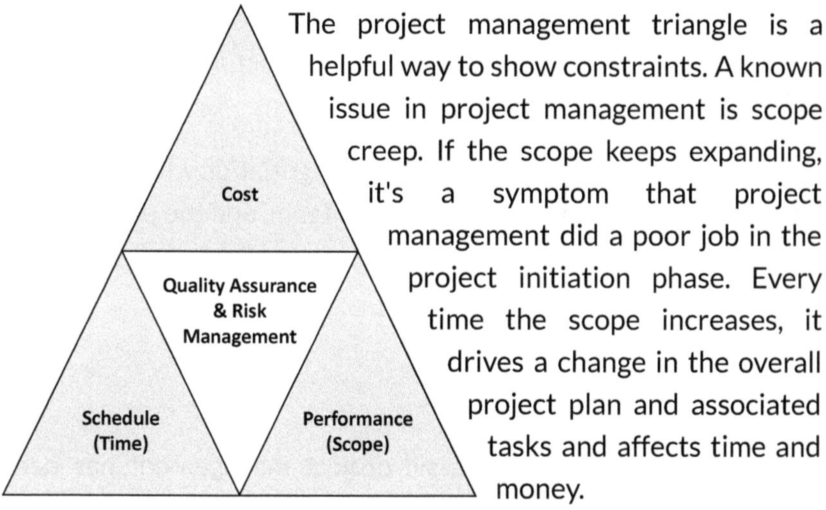

The project management triangle is a helpful way to show constraints. A known issue in project management is scope creep. If the scope keeps expanding, it's a symptom that project management did a poor job in the project initiation phase. Every time the scope increases, it drives a change in the overall project plan and associated tasks and affects time and money.

Time is finite. There will always be only 24 hours in a day. How you use that time is under your control. What happens during project execution is unpredictable in its effect on your time. For that reason, traditional project management techniques like adding slack in a task schedule to account for the unknown are an industry-accepted practice. Budgeting a cost buffer in the task to account for risk mitigation and quality assurance (performance) shortfalls is also accepted. These techniques will save time, and the more experienced the project manager is, the less likely it will be that cost, schedule, and performance constraints are violated.

Cost, schedule, and performance are a triad of project manager challenges. Project manager anticipation based on project management experience will define success or failure to keep within project parameters. If you anticipate well during project initiation (i.e., worst case scenario) and plan for it in the planning stage, you head off disaster.

The increasing power of computers to process data and information enables the project manager to keep more closely aware of how healthy the project is. Early predictions of project problems and risk probabilities help the project management head off project disruptions.

Open and realistic communication and negotiation with the project sponsors, essential stakeholders, client team, and the project team is crucial to success.

Waterfall method

Although the concept of classic project management has been changed and extended to accommodate many specialty purposes and methodologies, traditional notions are still considered the foundation for modern processes. That is a testament to traditional project management's ability to adapt and be flexible in its approach to managing projects. An excellent example is extending traditional project management to handle software projects. When you do that, you get the waterfall method of project management.

Waterfall adapts the traditional project management process where a project is broken down into distinct code modules and moved forward in sequential increments toward an ultimate objective. The individual modules are self-contained software code increments that each produce a final product function. As each sequential code module is delivered, it is linked together to create more and more capability until the software meets all the original requirements and functionality.

The project plan is created upfront in its entirety and then executed linearly. The completion of one section of code initiates the beginning of the next module of code. The key to project success is to devise a plan that will not change, and the software app is known from the beginning of the project.

The waterfall project management method inherited its characteristics from the traditional project management method. It's a once and done event from beginning to end. Each module of code is preplanned with all the integration hooks for past and future modules.

The stages of a waterfall correlate to those of a traditional project life cycle with different terminology in software speak.

- Requirements stage or task initiation
- Design stage or Planning
- Coding Stage or Execution
- Testing Stage or Monitoring and Control
- Deployment or project closing via a live demonstration. If the customer accepts the software, the project is over.

As you might expect, the Gantt chart that results from a waterfall project looks very much like a Gantt chart for a Traditional Project. It's a staircase, step-down looking chart that water would flow down the steps to completion.

Suitability

Using the Waterfall project management method for software development is risky. You must be 100% certain you know every detail about the software to be released. When delivery of one software module is late, each module downstream will be late as well. There is no slack in the schedule and nowhere to hide slush funds of cost to cover the delay.

The Waterfall project management method is suitable to use if:

- The software stands alone once done. There is no requirement to integrate it with other software.
- Your development team has done this work before and has the skills and experience needed to do it right the first time.
- The project does not require an iterative approach.
- Everything that needs to be done is low to no risk.
- The project has a hard deadline.
- The users cannot modify the code.

Traditional Project Management Example

The following serves as just one example of where traditional project management is a suitable solution for project delivery.

A webpage was to be delivered to a client. The delivery would merely be an addition to the current engagement between the customer and the company. The client had a specific set of requests for the solution, but not all requirements were available on the current platform.

All requirements were analyzed for fit or gap. Requirements that immediately fit the current platform were marked, and gaps were estimated in cost and time to deliver. The information was entered into a dialogue with the client that was limited in budget and schedule. An agreed set of specifications from the analyzed list was agreed to go into the delivery to fit both cost, time, and the optimal scope the customer could fit into the boundaries. A contract for the delivery was signed, thus moving the risk to the company delivering the solution.

Because of careful analysis and estimation of time and scope of the original list of requirements, the risk was acceptable to the company. The client was also happy with selecting a scope within boundaries and the upfront transparency of fit and gap. Not least was the solution delivered within a reasonable time from the agreed delivery date, the adjustments during deployment were negligible, and a clear end state of the project was possible. This could only happen because the company had detailed knowledge and previous experience solving similar challenges.

2. Agile Project Management

Agile project management is classic project management using fundamental practices of traditional combined with agile processes.

It is a traditional project methodology at the stakeholder level in which stakeholders see fixed costs and schedules. Simultaneously, clients can change the requirements using agile methods during project execution.

These values have made agile project management real by synthesizing agile methods in the same process as traditional methods.

The project management trend is that project managers must be fluent in more than one project methodology. You can see that trend in the more recent modern-day project management tools. They can do traditional planning and sprint planning using Kanban boards for those parts of the project that call for it. In most cases, the project manager can automatically create a Kanban board from a work breakdown structure developed for a traditional approach. No matter how big or small a project is, many simultaneous events are happening. Software tools are needed to do the planning and decision-making and maintain awareness and control of everything that's going on. The tools reduce the time necessary to plan and schedule projects. The visual graphing and charting techniques associated with Project Evaluation and Review (PERT) and Critical Path Management (CPM) accomplish that. The value gained becomes freeing up time for the project manager to concentrate on other essential project manager responsibilities has been such as resource, risk, and stakeholder management.

The project manager's job is to create a working interface between strategic and tactical operations. The integration and inclusion at the technical level are where the client's needs are served, whether that client is internally in the company or an external service. The customer wants to know all about cost, schedule, risk, and performance, the classic mandates of traditional project management.

A project manager is a manager of change. Implementation at the strategic level may be an entirely new business unit involving new leadership and significant HR challenges. At the tactical level, the business operations must create, test, and implement the associated processes. Change management at the tactical level is always a task of getting the entire business team to buy-in to new ways of working. Agile methods usually work better for the implementation part at the tactical level.

The Project Management Institute (PMI) has created the Program Management Book of Knowledge (PMBOK) that transcends all project management methodologies. PMBOK compiles the value-added processes, best practices, terminologies, and representative guidelines of completed projects. Structure and discipline, combined with a measure of flexibility, support the ability to adapt to changing requirements quickly. PMBOK separates the functions into three separate groups. The core functions define the structure of modern project management as they are always part of the process. There are times when other functions are needed to supplement the core functions. For that reason, some functions integrate into the modern project management process to provide the information needed to keep the core moving forward. Then, overarching functions glue everything together into one seamless progression that defines a successful project. Ten functions define the modern project management processes.

Core Functions of modern project management

Scope management

Consider agile principles as a means to an end. The customer is the source of everything that must be included in the project outcome. However, getting it right the first time is a pipe dream. Scope management is an iterative function, and that's what agile methods do well. Be it Scrum, brainstorming, or mind mapping, it doesn't matter. The critical thing is that input must be gathered from all stakeholders. The project manager and his team must define the scope and get buy-in from the corporate champion and the stakeholder sponsors. The iterations are never done until the scope is accepted and signed off by each entity in the approval chain. Planning doesn't start until the scope is accepted. The scope is still a dynamic document, however. Something will change, and the project manager must be ready to react and adjust. The project's scope will be in play for the duration of the project.

Quality Management

Quality Management is another part of the project process. Some will tell you quality has to be built-in upfront. It's a true statement, but it doesn't stop there. Requirements must be met, specifications must validate the requirements, and standards must be respected for the guidance they provide. Each project will have unique issues that must be dealt with, and it can be guaranteed that someone had done something similar before and documented their learnings, including learnings from those who have failed before. PMBOK makes it a point to learn from the past and incorporate those lessons in future releases of the project management process.

Time Management

Time impacts all phases of a project. Managing time goes towards cost, schedule, performance, and risk, translating into the project's responsible planning, estimates, schedules, and control tasks. Projects must have the innate ability to remain self-aware at all times. Project management tools are not only there to automate much of the hard work of project management; they are also there to wave the red flags and give off warning bells when something isn't going according to plan. The seasoned project manager will see the problem before the tools announce it.

Integrated Project Functions (External Influence)

These project management functions exist within the project's microcosm as part of the administration of contracts, human resources, internal and external communication, and risk mitigation. However, these functions' authoritative corporate responsibility lies external to the project. As such, the project moves forward with minimal attention to these functions. The project's success is enhanced if these corporate functions have a good working relationship with the project team.

Risk Management

The suggestion has already been made that risk management is a downplayed function of the project manager. It's one of the last things project managers will do because the function is a preparation for things that may never happen. However, the more successful and skilled project managers will give risk management its due because, if it happens, the project will most likely fail. There is a problem with the misleading nature of the concept of risk management. The word "management" suggests a way to control the risk events. However, setting up a slush fund to cover the unknown is neither art nor science. It's a hedge against the unknown with little evidence to support the need for it.

Human Resource Management

The project manager will have a close relationship with HR at the beginning of the project to find the skills and experience to do the work. The project manager's responsibility is to do this work within the project team. But, once the team is set, the need to meet with the authoritative corporate lead for HR melts away until someone leaves your team and you must replace that team member. You assume that since projects commit to an end, the team will see the work through until it's finished. The relationship with HR regresses to an on-call nature, and the project moves forward without them.

Contract/Legal Management

This project management issue is another case of the interface with the corporate department being needed upfront in the project initiation phase and then minimized once the project is executed. If you need help from this group, you ask for it when needed.

Communication Management

PMBOK assigns this as an integrated function. There is a strong case for moving this to the core functions group because of its importance in making sure the project keeps moving forward. The project champion will most likely be a corporate officer external to the project team. Many others in the C-suite will want to see periodic reports on the project's health and progress. Depending on your corporate environment, the project manager may want to have active communication with people external to the project at a more personal level.

Overarching Administrative Functions

Project Integration

The business structure and culture of the corporate organization is the primary issue. All projects within the company are born or die here. Corporate goals and objectives have an impact on what projects get funded or not. The project's corporate champion will make the business case in the board room. However, the project manager's role begins with creating that business plan and preparing a brief to support the project.

Strategic Planning

Once the project has cleared the boardroom with a green light for more extensive planning, the project manager will have to defend the work by ensuring the strategic plan supports corporate objectives. Money always gets tight on project work, and other project managers will not waste any time making sure their project gets the needed funds. The project manager will have to update briefs to the corporate hierarchy and address three levels of project importance:

1. Is the project technically innovative?
2. Is the schedule within reason and executable?
3. Are corporate assets being used in the most valuable way?

Resource Allocation

There are many decisions to be made regardless of the distribution of assets. People, money, and material are all on the table for discussion. Will material arrive in support of the project schedule? Do you have to develop a matrix plan to share project members with other projects? Do you have the critical skills available for your project? The answers to these questions become the decision factors that decide if the project gets into the master plan or not.

Suitability

Projects are filled with many simultaneous actions taking place. The complexity of staying self-aware is challenging for all projects. The hybrid nature makes it necessary for project managers to be fluent in both traditional and agile methods.

The agile project management method is suitable to use if:

- The overall project is within limiting boundaries.
- Overall, parts of the project feed into a sub-part of the project where the specification is not initially known.
- An iterative approach will give optimal results of delivering client needs.
- The risks are assessable, and a risk buffer can be agreed upon.
- The organization has skills in delivering agile project methods and risk management.
- The project's end state is clear, and there's a demand to meet the end-state and hand over the project outcome.

Hybrid Project Management Example

Below is an example of a hybrid approach to project management that embraces the agile manifesto's value: "Working software over comprehensive documentation" as well as providing the extensive documentation required to approve a medical device.

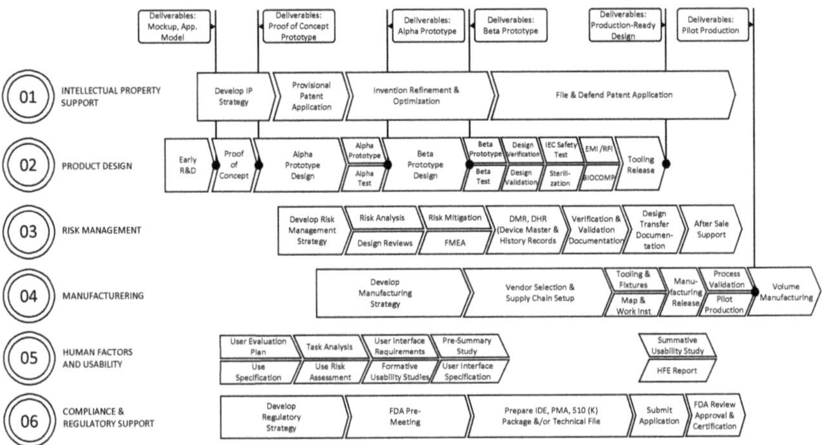

A project management approach such as this has been used in practice resulting in the approval of medical devices that meet regulatory requirements.

Hybrid management incorporates both agile software development and traditional documentation for quality assurance, requirements traceability, risk management, and electronic signatures where required.

Agile development methodologies improve product development economics by reducing costly and unnecessary project overhead to plan software features before the product needs are understood.

3. Agile Development

The "Manifesto for Agile Software Development", commonly referred to as "The Agile Manifesto", planted the seeds for agile as a philosophy and was immortalized in 2001.

Following the timeline, agile frameworks existed years before the publication of the Agile Manifesto. Some literature will falsely state that Scrum, Extreme Programming (XP), and others emerged from the Agile Manifesto, which is not entirely true. It is the other way around.

While not scribed into a set of stone tablets, it was published to the internet to a site that seems unchanged since 2001. The authors of the manifesto were a group of software engineers who held practical expertise in various software development processes such as XP, Scrum, Feature Driven Development, and other *pragmatic* ways of working and the traditional waterfall method.

While enjoying their mini-vacation in Snowbird, Utah, they started discussing their pain points with their experience using XP and various frameworks. They concluded they all shared common challenges and the same desire as to how they would like to work regardless of which framework is used for software development. They decided to write those ideas down as more of a symbolic gesture and never imagined it would start a movement commonly referred to as "agile development".

The resulting artifact became "The Agile Manifesto". While sounding extremely important and secretive, it is a simple set of statements written as four values and 12 supporting principles that describe the authors' public declaration of how they wish for organizations to balance people, collaboration, and process.

Manifesto for Agile Software Development

We are uncovering better ways of developing software by doing it and helping others do it. Through this work we have come to value:

Individuals and interactions over processes and tools
Working software over comprehensive documentation
Customer collaboration over contract negotiation
Responding to change over following a plan

That is, while there is value in the items on the right, we value the items on the left more.

The statements are simple enough, and no secret decoder ring is necessary to understand the intent.

For number one, the authors focused on people and how they work versus having processes and tools dictate or govern those interactions.

For example, using an agile lifecycle management tool such as Jira or VersionOne does not make you "agile". It does not make sense to create fancy Visio flowcharts of a process that does not enhance how people work. Or even worse, is designed to remove human interaction or trust between people.

Second, while documentation is important, our primary goal is to get software out the door faster instead of spending valuable time creating documentation the customer may not need. Sure, documents are necessary for compliance, sharing of information is important, like comments in one's code, but time is better spent on developing code.

Third, contract negotiation is reactive, and the outcome is to solidify a contract that becomes binding and rigid. For example, a legal contract or even a project plan could be considered a contract type. It is better to have conversations with the customer and collaborate early and often instead of referencing a contract that somehow becomes the holy grail of the work.

Lastly, responding to change over following a plan. It is a myth to believe that agile adoption means there are no plans. Plans are essential and happen all the time. In fact, in one of the most popular scaling frameworks, Scaled Agile Framework (SAFe), planning occurs often at all organization levels on a regular schedule. The mantra is "plan to replan" so that responding to change becomes effortless and frequent. Besides, many companies would no longer remain competitive if they weren't willing to replan often as necessary to meet their customers' needs faster and better than their competition.

The authors also created twelve underlying principles that support the four values. They are:

1. Our highest priority is to satisfy the customer through early and continuous delivery of valuable software.
2. Welcome changing requirements, even late in development. Agile processes harness change for the customer's competitive advantage.
3. Deliver working software frequently, from a couple of weeks to a couple of months, with a preference for the shorter timescale.

4. Business people and developers must work together daily throughout the project.
5. Build projects around motivated individuals. Give them the environment and support they need, and trust them to get the job done.
6. The most efficient and effective method of conveying information to and within a development team is face-to-face conversation.
7. Working software is the primary measure of progress.
8. Agile processes promote sustainable development. The sponsors, developers, and users should be able to maintain a constant pace indefinitely.
9. Continuous attention to technical excellence and good design enhances agility.
10. Simplicity--the art of maximizing the amount of work not done--is essential.
11. The best architectures, requirements, and designs emerge from self-organizing teams.
12. At regular intervals, the team reflects on how to become more effective, then tunes and adjusts its behavior accordingly.

When reading the value statements and principles, take note of any recommendation of a framework. Are you able to find any?

You will find no mention of any framework, process, or method hence why agile is closer to a philosophy than a methodology.

Why the "Agile Manifesto"?

Martin Fowler, one of the authors, describes the manifesto as a "rallying cry".

To understand the need for a "rallying cry", let's review at a high level the evolution of how software was developed in the early days of software programming versus today.

Early on, software developers were revered and respected for their knowledge. Maybe not equal to astronauts' celebrity status, but considering there was a lot of science, logic, math, and things most of us can't comprehend, there was a certain level of respect for software developers. Along with respect, a lot of trust.

Historically software was also something that took a long time to create, almost like a physical product, and did not necessarily need to change as often.

There were free and clear communication lines between the ones doing the work and their customers, which can also mean internal users of their software. This same environment is similar to what we witness in a start-up environment or entrepreneurship.

As software evolved into a more creative endeavor and the need for frequent innovation became more and more in demand, organizations began to add additional communication layers between developers and their customers.

As the divide between customer and developer further grew, stakeholders began to represent the customer, and project managers represented stakeholders.

Adding to the snowball that eventually caused the avalanche was a growing distrust between software developers and their customers. Instead of revered and respected, the perception of software developers became spoiled.

The typical reaction was to create more process and governance on top of existing processes or governance. The belief is that if there is more control, then one can control risk and uncertainty. The challenge is that developing software is emergent, creative, and very much filled with uncertainty.

The extra layers, control, and dogmatic methods created a false sense of control and ultimately encouraged bad behaviors such as ineffective command and control leadership styles. After all, *someone* had to monitor control over those strange unruly creatures living in the basement who were writing costly software code.

What typically could be solved in a conversation had to be represented as a task that lived somewhere within a detailed project plan that was driven by date and budget. Along with the date and budget constraint, the scope was also fixed.

Project plans became contracts between the software developers and the stakeholders. Once the plan was created, rarely was it adjusted even though the scope changed, or perhaps a developer won the lottery and never returned to complete their work. Unfortunately, progress was and is still measured by whether or not the pre-defined due date was met instead of whether something valuable was delivered to a customer.

In parallel, while companies were maturing, technology was changing.

Many years ago, software involved punch cards before the existence of electronic interfaces. In later times, programmable logic was used to crack German code in WWII and later help get the first man on the moon during the Apollo Mission.

In a not so long ago, a software update meant that something tangible was sent to a customer who installed the software update to their hardware. Now, updates are sent in seconds and are predominantly undetected by the customer.

The history of software development is fascinating. Even more fascinating is that a popular software development method, known as "waterfall", emerged around 1970 but did not quite evolve to be appropriate for developing the software we know today.

Unfortunately, the waterfall method was a misapplication or misunderstanding of an American computer scientist, Dr. Winston Royce's, recommendation he described in his 1970 paper, "Managing the development of large software systems ".

While he never used the term "waterfall", he described a sequential process model that outlined seven steps that he felt was appropriate for complex software development projects:

1. Systems Requirements
2. Software Requirements
3. Analysis
4. Program design
5. Coding
6. Testing
7. Operation

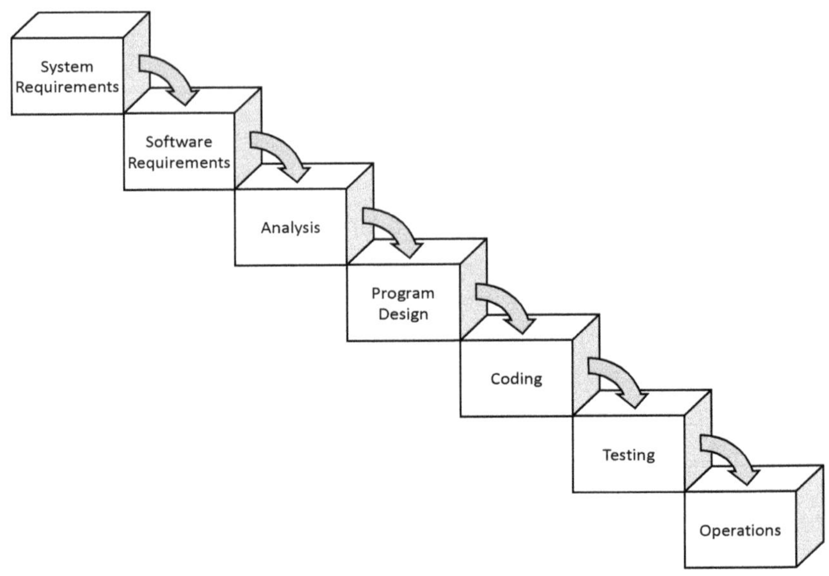

The supporting diagram appeared to represent a "waterfall"[1].

However, he did add that "the design iterations are never confined to the successive step", and a model without iteration is "risky and invites failure". He explained that it is difficult to analyze what happens in the testing phase precisely and that sometimes, you may need to go back to the drawing board and refactor your work or even your requirements. His warning was ignored.

For reasons we may never deeply understand, there was an attraction to the waterfall method for software development, and it slowly became widely adopted. And despite its downfalls, it is still a typical software development method used today. Perhaps because it was the only method available for about four years and four years is long enough to develop a long-term habit.

[1] http://www-scf.usc.edu/~csci201/lectures/Lecture11/royce1970.pdf

Concepts of more pragmatic and adaptive methods began to appear as early as 1974 when we began to see hints of an agile way of working, as we know it today.

Lightweight methods such as Scrum, Extreme Programming (XP), Crystal Methods, and Feature Driven Development had their opening acts starting in 1995.

It is important to note that these methods are based on human behavior studies from the 1950s. Some of the founders of those lightweight methods also authored the manifesto.

Despite these early introductions of agile methods, waterfall still took center stage from 1970 until the 2001 publication of The Agile Manifesto.

Agile Frameworks

Various frameworks fall under the agile philosophy realm, and more and more seem to emerge each year. The most common visual when describing agile is an umbrella with the names of the frameworks written underneath.

The most popular frameworks are Scrum and Kanban (a Lean Manufacturing model). Scrumban (a hybrid of Scrum and Kanban) and XP and Scrum hybrids are also popular. Value Stream Management (VSM), a method that optimizes steps necessary to deliver software and expose bottlenecks, is also gaining popularity.

While somewhat complicated to adopt because people are mainly resistant to change their familiar ways of working, these frameworks are popular because they are simple and are not meant to be heavy in terms of process or governance.

For scaling models, practices that extend beyond the development team level, Scaled Agile Framework (SAFe) is the most popular, followed by Scrum at Scale and LeSS. Many companies also reference the model made famous by Spotify, which, just as the name implies, is "*their*" model. According to Collabnet's 14th Annual State of Agile Report, there was an increase in SAFe adoption by 5% in 2019.

These agile frameworks, appropriate regardless of complexity, have practices that encourage collaboration, transparency, and iterative development. So, bug fixes, enhancements, new features, and products are delivered to the market faster.

As more and more companies experiment with different methods, they also adopt agile frameworks in other areas outside of software development. While the frameworks originated from software developers' experiences, adoption rates of those practices are increasing in many parts of the organization, such as marketing, supply chain, human resources, and finance.

Jeff Sutherland, one of the founders of Scrum and an author of the Agile Manifesto, has several videos available on his website, Scruminc.com, that shows how a team of people used Scrum to build a car.

Toyota began getting attention in the 80s when the world noticed they were building cars more efficiently and better than their American competitors. Taiichi Ohno, an industrial engineer at Toyota, developed a pull-system focused on flow and just-in-time production. We call this system Kanban. You may witness Kanban in action every day, such as ordering food at a restaurant.

Regardless of industry, more and more organizations are starting to become agile while others are just getting started.

Agile Transformation

An agile transformation is the marriage of agile as a philosophy and adoption of agile frameworks that, when combined and balanced, become embedded as part of an entire organization's culture. Gradually, practices and behaviors start to appear at all levels of an organization from CEO to team level or sometimes team level UP to the CEO. We commonly refer to this as the agile ecosystem.

One of the most cited reasons for embarking on a transformation is delivering faster to market. The organization realizes the need to be nimble and react to the customer's needs quickly and better than their competition.

Organizations recognize the need to not only deliver faster but also deliver the right products and solutions to their customers. Of course, by delivering faster to the market, feedback returns faster, giving the organization the ability to improve their products continuously, thereby reducing the risk of building the wrong product or, worse, the right product riddled with defects.

Attracting and retaining talent is another top reason organizations want to transform. Agile empowers people and provides an environment in which people can be autonomous and innovate, improving morale. Google, for example, is a popular agile organization. People do not necessarily get excited to work for a search engine; they get excited because of the culture.

Agile is a change in the organization's decision authority, moving decision-making to where the information is, which in most technical matters and many customer-related matters means away from higher-level management to lower organization levels.

Changing away from a known authority hierarchy is a complex challenge.

Mixed Models

Most organizations ready to transform their organizations to reflect agile ways of working will typically bring in teams of Agile Coaches who will help the organization develop a path towards transformation. Agile Coaches bring in the knowledge and practical experience to help an organization navigate the bumps and potholes they will become exposed to during their journey.

As a starting point and even long-term, it is not uncommon to see a mix of Scrum, Kanban, and hybrid models such as Scrumban or Agile-Fall within an organization in the early phases of transformation.

The variations in methods are mainly because not one size fits all in every situation. Whether it be the type of work or agile maturity of the people or the organization, it may be necessary to experiment with different frameworks and variations.

Suppose you pluck away some of the aspects of waterfall that are no longer needed, such as managing cost, schedule, and scope; there is still a need for some traditional activities in harmony with the agile transformation. It is not that all management activities suddenly go away in an agile world; they are just done differently. Examples are managing product features, priority, risk, stakeholder, communication, and deployment, which are still relevant in an agile organization.

If the type of work that needs to be done can be clearly defined upfront and there will be less variation in the final output, it may easier to adhere to a traditional planning method. Traditional project management is better suited for more predictable work where there's a high consistency once the build process begins.

Modern software development is a creative type of work, and one cannot always identify the exact outputs regardless of how solid the requirements. There is a strong need to adapt due to rapid technological advancements and customer needs. Agile accepts higher variability and welcomes change even late in the build process.

But any mix of methods might be valid, depending on the specific organization. A mixed model is beneficial during transformation and in large organizations with varying initiatives.

Many refer to interim states as a "hybrid" model where some traditional practices still exist while the organization moves towards agile transformation and adoption.

Even a closer look at agile practices, there will be a mix of Scrum, Kanban, XP, Test Driven Design, Pair Programming, and other practices we don't generally read about when doing an internet search of "agile".

It is also advisable that certain conditions should be met before massive changes are rolled out in some parts of an organization. While this may sound vague or cryptic, Agile Coaches are experienced in forming these strategies and timing those changes.

In other words, companies should not just eliminate all project managers the day they decide to "go agile". The project manager role is transformed to a servant leader role with impediment removal, coordination with vendors, managing dependencies, and budget monitoring, to name a few. Some activities will slowly go away. For example, reports are generated based on empirical data, updated in real-time, and accessible to all.

Funding still needs to be allocated, monitored, and controlled, but it becomes easier when the organization begins to align people to long-lived teams. Accounting also slowly moves away from traditional cost center funding to team funding and lean budgets. Metrics may need to be reviewed and evolve to ensure they drive value.

Unless the organization is a start-up and does not suffer from the complexities of large organizations, none of these changes happen overnight. It takes time to adjust not only practices but also to prepare those who are involved.

Ultimately, success will depend on people's willingness to try something new and experiment; after all, it is people first, practices second.

Suitability

While never monetized or heavily marketed, the Agile Manifesto became popular quickly and can be given credit for shedding light on the lesser-known frameworks. However, if we understand the intent, we realize that the practices were not enough; the "rallying cry" was to put the focus back on the humans doing the work.

Don't Let History Repeat Itself

Einstein is famously credited for saying that insanity is doing the same thing repeatedly and expecting a different result.

Just as Dr. Royce's "Managing the development of large software systems" paper was misunderstood, the Agile Manifesto can also be misunderstood and misapplied.

Dr. Royce expressed his thoughts and cautioned against a sequential process, yet all that seemed to stand out was the waterfall image that depicted a sequence.

The Agile Manifesto authors essentially ask for the focus to return to collaboration and not allow management control to stifle innovation and creativity.

Yet, many organizations misunderstand the intent behind the message and the impact it was meant to have. Agile transformation is bound for failure if there is an expectation that "agile" is another "sequential process" that will magically fix all the organization's pain points.

One can "be agile" and never follow a framework,
just as one can "do Scrum" and never "be agile".

The agile development method is suitable to use if:

- The team is working on the same product.
- The team is expected to be working continuously.
- New features and functions will be requested at the same rate as previously requested features are delivered.
- The team is working together as a group.
- The entire team must work on the same projects/features, not split between projects/features within the team)
- The team can benefit from owning a process, end-to-end, preferably including support of the live product
- The team is a long-standing team.
- There's no end-state or delivery of a final product to satisfy a contract.

Agile development Example

Below is an example of a setting that has a perfect fit with the agile delivery model.

A company is selling software services to their customers. The offer is a license for using the service, and the contract includes both new development and support of the live system. Each customer buys from hundreds to thousands of seats for their workforce.

Depending on the volume, the customer has a considerable influence on prioritizing the backlog of customer-requested features. However, it is ultimately up to the company to decide what to work on, as there may be factors that customers do not have the insight they need to decide on.

The company creates several different teams for different final product areas. One team's product is databases and integrations, and another team's product is front-end user experience. Other teams handle different responsibilities of the whole system, like financial models, budget and invoicing, platform management, and first-line communication with customers.

The overall product is governed by a lean process of evaluating new requirements and ensuring the delivery provides value to the customers. Each team works with short-term goals to deliver incremental value and handle their product end-to-end, including supporting their live environment deliveries.

This setting is the classical value proposition for selecting an agile delivery model.

4. Lean Operation

Lean manufacturing is a widely recognized and practiced business philosophy in today's Industry environments. To those who already know the basic principles of Lean, it will come as no surprise that most industries use some variation of Lean principles. In a 2015 survey of 25,000 businesses by Compdata, 71% had applied Lean in some way[1].

Lean philosophy's basic concept is to maximize what the customer finds of value while minimizing waste. Another way of stating this philosophy: "Lean" means creating optimal value while utilizing the fewest resources.

By using concepts of process standardization, reducing complexity, and improving flexibility, a business can focus on what the customer wants. They can select the improvement methodologies that best achieve customer satisfaction while minimizing the organization's resources to the smallest amount possible.

While examples of effective utilization of Lean methodologies are easily found throughout multiple manufacturing environments, it would be a misconception to believe that Lean is limited to manufacturing environments. Lean applies to every process of many businesses and organizations that produce and provide goods or services. Besides being implemented in production and manufacturing environments, it has been used in healthcare, banking, finance, insurance companies, and government

[1] https://www.mmh.com/article/how_manufacturing_employers_are_getting_lean

institutions. An Insight Survey completed in June of 2020, 77% of those surveyed were in the services/transactional industry[1].

Therefore, Lean Philosophy has a valuable role in multiple departments within a given service industry, not only production. What department would not benefit from the elimination of waste in their processes? Yes, the Lean Philosophy is valuable for entire organizations by eliminating wastes not only in isolated parts of a process but along an entire organization's value streams for any value-added process.

Change can be challenging, and becoming genuinely Lean requires a considerable amount of time and effort. Experiencing disputes within the team or among the process owners when a team is to improve a process is expected. This clash will make the team's success difficult to achieve and should be anticipated; best practice deals with disagreement in an open and honest discussion where all voices can be heard.

While many organizations pursue continuous improvement, incidences of attempted application can provide some minimal improvement or reduction of waste. To truly become a Lean Environment, to maximize benefits, taking a holistic approach and making the Lean Philosophy a core company principle is necessary. All participants in the organization shall learn to apply a Lean approach that enhances improvement by providing this philosophy as a core value.

Lean organizations and supply chains' characteristics are described in the book *Lean Thinking*, first published in 1996 by Jim Womack

[1] https://goleansixsigma.com/lean-six-sigma-industry-insight-survey

and Dan Jones, founders of the Lean Enterprise Institute and the Lean Enterprise Academy (UK), respectively. The authors argue that a Lean way of thinking allows companies to "specify value, line up value-creating actions in the best sequence, conduct these activities without interruption whenever someone requests them, and perform them more and more effectively".

Origins of Lean

The term "lean" was coined to describe Toyota's business during the late 1980s by a research team headed by Jim Womack, Ph.D., at MIT's International Motor Vehicle Program. Originally called "Just in Time Production", it was embodied in what Toyota called "The Toyota Way", an improvement methodology. Taiichi Ohno and Eiji Toyoda, Japanese industrial engineers who worked for Toyota's automotive group, developed the system between 1948 and 1975. Originally rich in the philosophy of the complete elimination of all waste (Muda), Lean has evolved through many years of trial and error to improve efficiency while reducing waste. Waste in a corporation can manifest in many ways. The Lean Philosophy defines seven possible types of waste to evaluate for elimination.

1. Transport	Unnecessary movement of products.
2. Inventory	All components, work in progress, and finished product (i.e., all materials not currently being processed).
3. Motion	People or equipment moving or walking more than is required to perform processing.

4. Waiting	Waiting for the next operational step in the process (e.g., waiting on a patient to show up, waiting within service industries).
5. Over-production	Producing ahead of demand and other inefficient uses of capacity.
6. Over Processing	Overprocessing resulting from poor tool or product design creating activity.
7. Defects	Effort spent with inspecting for and fixing defects.

Lean transformation is not accomplished fast. A company's transformation into genuine Lean is a journey, not an endpoint. Companies should strive for continuous improvement and the continual elimination of waste. Organizations that have embraced Lean Philosophy have transformed themselves into a group of collective Lean practitioners who continuously strive to identify and remove waste.

Five Principles of Lean

Lean encourages continuous improvement by reducing waste, adding value to the customer, and being based on respect for people. The five principles of Lean are considered a recipe for improving workplace efficiency and include: 1) defining value, 2) mapping the value stream, 3) creating flow, 4) using a pull system, and 5) pursuing perfection.

Defining Value

It is essential to understand what value is. Value is what the customer is willing to pay for. The customer may not know what they want or cannot articulate what they need. Lean Philosophy tools such as interviews, surveys, demographic information, and data validation can help a company decipher and discover what customers find valuable.

Value Stream Mapping

In value stream mapping, the goal is to use the customer's value as a reference point and identify all the activities contributing to these values. Activities that are non-value-add activities are considered waste. The waste can be broken into non-value adding but necessary and non-value & unnecessary. For example, in a heat-treating operation, a manufacturer may choose to batch many parts to fill the oven. If parts are waiting for an oven to be filled, this is considered a required but non-value-added activity. By reducing and eliminating unnecessary processes, a company can provide the customer exactly what they value while at the same time reducing the cost of producing that product or service. A patient coming to a doctor's office for nothing more than an Influenza vaccination and being required to see both the nurse and the physician is an example of non-value and unnecessary activity. Yes, a physician order is required, but the physician can create standing orders allowing the nurse to work to the top of their license to evaluate the safety of administering that day and proceed with the vaccine.

Creating Flow

After removing waste from the value stream, the next step is to understand the flow of product, service, or material and information flow. Some strategies for ensuring that value-adding activities flow smoothly include: breaking down steps, reconfiguring the production / or process steps, leveling out the workload, creating cross-functional departments, and cross-training employees to become multi-skilled and adaptive.

Establishing a Pull Environment

Inventory is one of the most extensive forms of waste in any organization. A pull-based system's goal is to limit inventory and work in process. And still provide materials and information available for a smooth flow of work. A pull-based system allows for Just-in-time delivery where products or services are created when needed and in the quantities needed. By starting at the end of the value stream and working backward through the production system, we can ensure that the products or services produced will satisfy customers' needs. The hamburger chain that advertises you can "have it your way" in theory only makes the next burger when the customer "pulls" and places their order.

Pursue Perfection

The fifth step of pursuing perfection is the most important among them all. It makes the Lean Philosophy and continuous process improvement a part of the organizational culture. Every participant in the organization will strive towards perfection while delivering products based on the customer's needs and always find ways to get a little better every day.

Lean Toolbox

Implementing a Lean Philosophy requires a practical understanding of many tools and templates; however, Kaizen, 5S, Kanban, Value Stream Mapping, and PDCA are among the most useful lean tools.

Kaizen

Kaizen leverages knowledge and ingenuity from every employee, every person on a project team, organizational subject matter experts, and especially the "Doers" of the process. Commonly known as "Kaizen Events", they are designed to create rapid workplace change. They target specific areas that need to be improved deliberately over several days to make dramatic changes in a short period of time.

5S

The 5S tool is designed to improve efficiency through a systematic approach to organization and cleanliness in the workplace. It includes five fundamental guidelines (five S's) that help improve workplace efficiency. The five S's are Sort, Set, Shine, Standardize, and Sustain. 5S makes workplaces more efficient and effective by:

- Removing unneeded items from each work area *(Sort)*
- Customizing each unique work area to maximize efficiency *(Set)*
- Cleaning work areas at the end of all shifts *(Shine)*
- Documenting work instructions so they can be easily followed *(Standardize)*
- Ensuring each step is completed consistently to ensure continuous improvement *(Sustain)*

Kanban

Kanban is a visual production system that makes sure Doers have what they need, where they need it, and when they need it. Kanbans use a visual signal to indicate when the Doer requires more materials. Using Kanbans, the organization can more easily manage inventory and reduce unneeded stock. This allows reacting to actual needs instead of making guesses to anticipate future needs, thus reducing waste and improving efficiency.

Value Stream Mapping

Value Stream Mapping (VSM) is a visual lean tool that helps identify process steps across a value stream. Typically used to analyze the current process, highlight waste or hidden factories, and then create what can be referred to as a "Future State". Hidden factories are steps that are not part of the formalized work plan but are performed by the Doers. They may be valuable steps that only the Doer as a subject matter expert knows to include. Through VSM, all new or updated processes are represented by an updated visual map, allowing improvement to continue.

PDCA

It is an acronym for the Plan-Do-Check-Act cycle. This lean tool's strength comes from its clear, no-nonsense steps. Its purpose is to provide a structure that guides problem-solving and process improvement. This approach establishes a comprehensive feedback loop to ensure success. First, a problem is defined (Plan), then analyzed (Do). In the "check" step, validate with data that the root cause has been identified. Next is the action plan, but the intent is never to stop there, but instead go back to the cycle's beginning.

Where to Begin

Once a Manager or Supervisor has been trained and understands Lean Philosophy, how and where should they begin their implementation? They understand the Principles of Lean and have a working knowledge of Lean Tools. Leadership now expects them to successfully lead a team to reduce waste in the organization's processes but is it clear how to begin?

These Lean Management tips may help a Manager or Supervisor get started.

Value Stream Ownership

Make sure every value stream has someone responsible for overseeing the flow of each process step within the value stream. This individual should also have a strong understanding of the customers' expectations for the value stream's goods or services. A question for these individuals to ask themselves is, "How can I make customers happy with fewer resources by engaging the full energies of our people to improve this value stream?" Using input from the Doers of the processes will help identify value-added process steps and non-value-added activities.

Focus on the process

It is better to steer clear of complex metrics and measures. If Value Stream Owners focus on productivity, the process is likely never to improve. In most cases, production measures come at the end of the process, where the waste has already materialized. Using Lean Tools like Plan, Do, Check, Act, (PDCA) Value Stream Owners and the Doers can effectively identify and remove waste.

Communicate

Let's consider the multitude of reasons why it is essential to keep your organization informed of your goals, expectations, and successes. First is the importance of communicating with leadership. They will need to be informed of any identified needs involving capital expenditure or subject matter expert support (e.g., IT, Procurement). They will also want to be made aware of successes in removing waste as after adjusting any internal costs in the goods or service, sales margins will likely change.

Second, make sure all involved understand you are focused on the process, not individual performance. This will facilitate better engagement with subject matter experts and Doers, which will improve the ability to succeed.

Lastly, success is to be celebrated. All individuals want to be good performers and appreciate being able to celebrate success. This will help foster that a Lean Philosophy is a part of the organization's culture and core beliefs.

Lean Management

The Lean Philosophy, Phases of Lean and Lean Tools are excellent ways to improve your organization continuously. Just as a writer must have a vision of what is to be written on paper before the pen or quill can benefit the writer, the writer must understand the process of creating incredible works of literature.

One who seeks to implement Lean Management must understand the value stream of their organization, the customer's value, and make continuous improvement a core belief of their organization.

A Lean Practitioner early in their introduction to Lean Philosophy would typically be initially trained with peers as a group in the application of Lean. Then that group would be divided into teams to focus on processes that have an opportunity for improvement by reducing waste. After gaining experience in Lean Philosophy, the team members would have the opportunity to lead and participate in other projects. There are many project types available for the practical application of Lean. Some projects may be structured around a value stream and managed within a project plan. Others may be structured around the Kaizen philosophy of small incremental but continuous improvement. And still, others may be a Kaizen Blitz, focused on specific actions taken in a relatively short period of time and concluded rapidly. In each instance, these applications focus on removing waste in a process by applying the principles we are about to discuss.

*"If this Lean stuff seems easy,
you're probably not doing it."* [1]

A Lean team's desire for change can be strong, and change may still be elusive. That is why the Lean Leader will want to start with a discussion with their team about a vision of effectively removing waste. This vision should undergird all conversations and plans and consistently improve value streams. By validating the aspiration to embrace this philosophy of incremental improvement, teams will be more likely to forgo a swing for the fence's mentality of sweeping change but rather be resolute in embracing the Lean Philosophy vision.

[1] Womack, J., Jones, D., Roos, D. (1991) Lean and the Machine that Changed the World

Project Charter

When beginning to apply a Lean Philosophy, the practitioner should define what they expect to accomplish and communicate this to all value stream levels. This is done using a project charter. A project charter is typically a short document that describes the project and formally authorizes activities to begin. Each section is required to be complete and approved by the project champion:

Problem Statement	*Defines the problem so that the project team and stakeholders can focus their attention on solving the problem.*
Business Case	*Identifies the business need for the project and describes its relationship with the organization's high-level strategic goals.*
Goal Statement	*States the desired results of a process improvement project.*
Project Scope	*Defines what is in scope as deliverables for the project and what is out of scope.*
Team/Roles	*Defines who will be on the team, and their roles will be based on skills and abilities.*
Measures	*Documents baseline as well as target metrics and customer requirements.*
Milestones	*Defines the project plan and scheduled activities.*
Champion	*The champion is the authorizing individual with ultimate responsibility for the project. Typically, a member of the leadership team.*

When leading a group or team through the project, the leader will often start each team meeting with a quick review of the project charter to keep all team members aligned and limit scope creeps to the best of the team's ability. Once the champion has approved the project charter, it should not be changed. If a change is believed necessary, it is critical to review and change both the scope and the deliverable.

DMAIC

In addition to the PDCA Tool (Plan-Do-Check-Act cycle) that provides a structure for problem-solving, another tool is used to apply Lean Philosophy; It goes by the acronym DMAIC (pronounced duh-mā-ick). DMAIC represents the cycle of Define-Measure-Analyze-Improve-Control.

Define

In the first step, Define, the team will define and state the problem, identify the customer requirements, at a high-level map the process, identify output measures, and identify the potential benefits of improving the process. Once this is complete, this phase of the cycle will be reviewed for approval with the project champion to advance to the next step.

Measure

In the second step, Measure, the team will add detail to the process map, identify all input variables, develop a data collection plan, capture process capabilities, determine potential improvements, and establish improvement goals. The importance in this step of "real" and "quantifiable" data cannot be overemphasized. Often teams fail to improve because they followed a plan instead of following the data. A project review & approval are needed before advancement to the Analyze step in the cycle.

Analyze

In step three, prioritize the input variables and identify root causes of undesired variables, use data to validate the team's findings, and select the root cause to address that will have the most significant impact. In this step of Analyze, be clear to focus on the process and not individual performance. As with the previous steps, review & approval are required to advance to the Improve step.

Improve

In the fourth step, Improve, the team will establish relationships between the selected root cause and output measures identified in the first step, develop an improvement plan for the selected root cause, and implement a pilot to validate improvements. It is critical in this step that all team members shall have equal status when it comes to input, and silent objectors should be drawn out and allowed a voice. Remember to review & approve before advancing to the Control step.

Control

In the fifth step, Control, the team will develop controls around the improvement, validate the benefits with the improvement, document the outcomes, identify where the improvement translates to other opportunities in the value stream, and develop an audit plan for continued performance. Upon approval of this final step in the cycle, the team should acknowledge and celebrate the project's success.

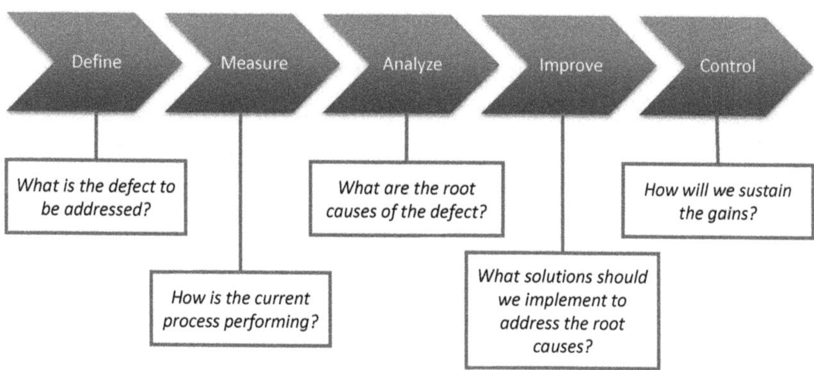

The DMAIC cycle involves change. It will most likely change how a business process is performed, how it is measured, and how it is controlled. Not all doers of the process will embrace change, underscoring why "real" and "quantifiable" data is required. It is easier to bring along reluctant doers when an improvement plan is validated with data.

Factors that Impact Application

Many factors may impact a team's success or failure in applying Lean Philosophy. Some Lean Philosophy application tools are common to most improvement methodologies, such as Lean, Six Sigma, and Total Quality Management.

Here are five frequently used methodologies that can lead to a successful project when applied within the DMAIC cycle.

Root Cause Analysis

Root cause analysis is a collective term that describes an approach and technique to uncover causes of problems. Those responsible for completing the process and experiencing an issue should be a part of the root cause discussion. Significance is placed on defining the problem, brainstorming its possible causes, analyzing causes and effects, and suggesting solutions to the problem. Remember, in most cases, the simplest solution can be the most productive. NASA research spent thousands of dollars trying to create an ink pen to be used in zero gravity. After countless hours with no success, they learned that Russian cosmonauts used pencils.

Standard Work

Standard work is creating, communicating, and tirelessly following standards. In the mapping of processes in Define and Measure steps, one should validate standards for the process and assure that they are being followed. Standard work will provide stability and consistency that will help to avoid waste.

Hospitals began seeing fewer errors when they instituted "Standard" checklists, following the safety examples of aircraft pilots in pre-flight check.

Mistake Proofing

Mistake Proofing is a process improvement tool used to prevent or detect a specific error from occurring or reoccurring. An error in this context is any deviation from standard work. Mistake Proofing will also Correct problems as soon as they are detected to prevent additional wastes. Mistake Proofing notifications come in two signals.

- Warnings that provide information about an error that is about to occur.
- Controls that will stop the process when an error occurs.

Word processing spell check, retail barcodes, and pharmaceutical childproof packaging are all forms of Mistake Proofing.

Process Mapping

A Value Analysis Process Map is a diagnostic tool that looks at each process step to identify which steps provide value to the customer.

- Value Added process steps are essential to delivering products or services according to customer requirements.
- Value Required process steps are not adding value to the product but are nevertheless required to meet customer requirements.
- Non-Value-Added process steps do not qualify as value-adding or value required. Non-value-added activity in the process should be identified as waste.

An example of a Value Analysis Process Map can be creating flow charts, swimlane diagrams, and data flow diagrams.

Visual Signals

Visual signals alert when action or information is required. To provide benefit close to the process, visual signals should be understood by the doers of the process and provide enough detail at a glance so the action can be taken.

- Visual Identifiers like signal lights, arrows, floor markings, and color-coding trigger an action without labels or signs.
- Visual Instructions like signs, maps, pictures similarly trigger an action or clarify when an action is prohibited.
- Visual Measure examples include displaying current productivity, displaying the standard productivity, or a project management board.

Leaders of Lean

Lean leadership is necessary for creating a successful Lean Philosophy. The Lean Leader must be effective in helping their team embrace a culture of continuous improvement. This can be difficult. A team is a group of individuals with unique perspectives and varying levels of emotional investment in "the way things have always been done."

Beyond leading the team to understand and use the philosophies and tools of Lean, the leader must also build a team that has a clear vision of the value of continuous improvement for the value stream as a whole. The team will ideally view the leader as totally committed to the vision and capable of objectivity about the data.

There are three key attributes that a Lean Leader should possess to build and lead a successful project team effectively. By possessing and demonstrating these attributes, the Lean Leader will be a better leader.

Be Relatable to the Team

The Lean Leader should express or relate their vision as something that every member of the team can easily understand. They should feel excited to be a part of the team and personally commit.

The team will follow the leader only when they feel the leader believes in what they are doing will profoundly improve the work environment.

An example of a leader being relatable to the team from the aviation industry:

> A VP of Operations (John "Cub" Marion) asked all of his direct reports to create a personal "Credo" that drives them. Each direct report was given a chance to deliver their ideology at a weekly operations meeting. All were inspiring, some even to the point of tears. The final ideology presented was Cub's ideology. After this exercise, team members reported feeling a bond with Cub and an urge to perform at their best for the company.

Be the Most Positive Person in the Room

Another attribute to being a genuinely great Lean Leader is positivity. Positivity will energize everyone in the room and allow them to approach challenging issues with inspiration. Positivity will also help the team see challenges as opportunities instead of obstacles. Practicing positive thinking can be so contagious that it can change the atmosphere of the environment for the whole team:

> A manager in an engineering department was concerned about department morale in the 2007 era of recession and layoff notices and department shrinkage. At a weekly Team Leader meeting, the Manager requested the department to begin an exercise in positive thinking reminiscent of encouraging his child every night "Hey, let's have the best day ever tomorrow." When greeted by anyone in the department, he asked his team to respond with, "I am having the best day ever."
>
> It took a while for the catchphrase to become part of the departmental culture. Still, some months later, upon entering a meeting room and giving the team a "Morning guys, how are we?" he was delighted with a resounding chorus of "Having the best day ever" from all forty-seven engineers in the room. This department still had workload complications, but they were a team that started from a place of positivity.

Be Present for Your Team

During the project, a team member may ask for personal attention in general mentoring, problem solving, or managing peer relationships. This is a sign of trust the team member has in the leader and confidence in their judgment. When a Lean leader is available for personal conversations, it signals to the team members their value and importance to their success. Authenticity is a gift that may pay dividends on the current project or in the future.

> A newly promoted lead consulted a supply chain manager about a disgruntled employee complaint. Having worked with this lead on past Lean projects, she was inspired by how the man interacted with his peers. This positive interaction was a factor in her promotion of him. She thus knew he could handle the complaint and only needed to get past his initial fears. She brought up a type of leader she respects: "the tough but fair teacher" from school days. After a bit, the leader stated, "You know, just talking about and thinking of Mrs. __ [from his school days] makes me confident I can handle this."

Project Closure

A last but crucial part of Lean Philosophy is celebrating project success. Leadership should know the success they sponsored has been realized, and your team should feel proud of their work and energized for the next project. Maybe most importantly, the doers of the process should feel they had a voice in the change, and Lean Philosophy brought value to the value stream.

Now, what's our next project?

Suitability

Lean operational methods are suitable to use if:

- The tasks are repetitive.
- The tasks are similar in size.
- The tasks come in large numbers.
- The work is or resembles a production line.
- Each step in the process can be defined and documented and are not varied in terms of acceptance criteria and quality delivery.
- The process has a clearly defined start trigger and outcome.
- The process is internal and under your control to improve if needed.
- It is possible to collect precise measurements of each step in the process.
- There's value in improving the process.

Lean Operation Example

Nine bottles are being packaged as a monthly tasting box at a warehouse. The tasting box is sent to thousands of subscribed clients each month. Every month is nine new bottles being shipped.

The process is a heavy task for three persons over a week's curse. The process involves unpacking hundreds of boxes of each bottle and packing thousands of subscriber boxes with nine bottles before shipping.

The DMAIC problem-solving method is used to analyze the process. Through meticulous going in the process's footsteps (Gemba), every detail of the process is measures and documented. Diagrams of workplaces are registered, and movement is being timed. All waste (Muda) is registered. And a value stream map (VSM) of the current process is drawn with timings of process and stock time per unit in the workflow.

The consequences of each waste found in the process are established, and improvement ideas for each consequence are recorded. Improvements are group and estimated for impact and effort. Ideas with low effort and high impact are considered first, while ideas with high effort and low impact are discarded right away. Some improvements are costly, so cost-benefit is also analyzed. A possible future Value Stream Map of the improved process is drawn, and impact is estimated.

Each improvement is selected for implementation. After each implementation, the effect is measured to validate the improvement, and outcomes are documented.

5. PAPAO management model

In the previous chapters, we have explored four different areas of managing large initiatives:

- ❑ P Projects
- ❑ AP Agile Projects
- ❑ A Agile development
- ❑ O Operation

This chapter will explore how to connect these four management areas and see that these are not excluding. These are areas in which all companies must navigate and put the relevant framework to use where applicable. Interoperability between the areas is crucial to effectiveness, which we will explore at the end of the chapter.

Let us explore the differences between these four management areas from a lifespan and experience perspective.

Lifespan

Lifespan is the perceived length of time the initiative is supposed to continue developing the product. In particular, how long the organization is expected to continue when you start the initiative. And for this purpose, the essential point is whether there is an expected end of the initiative. Or whether it is expected to continue until the market demands a change.

One-time Projects

A project's goal is the handover, which means delivering value to the customer. The project team delivers proper documentation and training, and the delivery goes into operation. The project team supports the product during a short hyper-care period, after which the customer takes over the continuous ownership and maintenance of the delivery. The project organization is dissolved and ventures into new projects.

In projects where a customer takes over the delivery, the project is eager to create a clearly defined cutover, benefiting both organizations. The delivery team can be released to new projects, and the customer formally starts taking value from the delivery, as would be the case with physical construction work. In agile projects, customers have been an integral part of the project; thus, the transition is faster and less of a burden for both the delivering and the receiving team.

There's no difference between traditional projects and hybrid projects from a lifespan perspective. Both have well-defined end criteria, which we are looking for when assessing lifespan. A hybrid project has a clearly defined scope, budget, and timeline, even though the actual work isn't agreed upon until it is needed. Many current projects are handled like this, as we have seen in the chapters on hybrid project management. An example is a campaign of some sort. The campaign would know the end date and the budget to achieve as much value as possible. Or could be asked to achieve a certain quality within an end date, whatever the cost. Within the project boundaries, the work can be agreed upon in any way needed and will evolve as the team learns and sets goals for the coming increments.

Continuity of Operation

Operation is the management of continuous delivering and optimizing value in the marketspace. This includes setting up lean processes, optimizing the cost of supporting the product. Support includes incident management and root cause problem solving that may emerge over time when the product is released to the market. The product will eventually have to be updated, which calls for managing new requirements and releasing changes to the market. Continuous service management, including availability, capacity and performance management, and many other practices, exists to manage to get value from the product. Many of these processes involve continuous lifecycles and should always be a case for continuous optimization and relentless improvement. Luckily as we have seen in the past chapters, there's a myriad of good practices to make sure we can measure, plan and predict optimization efforts.

At a certain point, a product becomes obsolete and is discontinued or surpassed by better or cheaper products and thus no longer is viable. Operations take care of closing down existing products when their lifespan is over or kick off a reinvention creating a new project to revamp the product to compete with the market evolution. The key to operations is that it doesn't have a set end date when introduced. The end date becomes apparent through proper management of the product. One can argue that some products have a set lifespan and thus end date, which is true. Still, those can be perceived as campaigns that will resemble projects more than operation, managed with milestones, accomplishments, metrics of success and failure, and decision points.

The difference between projects and operations is lifespan. Projects have a well-defined ending. Operations are continuous.

Continuity of Agile development

The biggest problem often faced is to define an end state clearly. Some deliveries tend to go on "forever" because there are areas to improve and new requirements to be implemented.

A modern fix is the "you build it – you run it" approach that many companies adopt. This approach applies especially if the delivery is within the same organization. Operation stays with the same relative group of people developing that will also handle the product's ongoing improvement. This approach is common in agile organizations.

It will come as no surprise that the idea behind agile development is continuous, whether or not the agile organization handles operation or not. It is not the possible operation in agile organizations that make them continuous, but the idea that the organization doesn't strive to finalize the product development; rather, the product is perceived as continuously evolving.

As we have seen in previous chapters, projects like physical construction work can't be taken as a continuous agile development as the end state needs to be clear from the beginning. However, developing software products fit into the idea of continuous development, but the thought of continuous development isn't limited only to software products. Hardware technology evolves continuously and can undoubtedly benefit from agile development in terms of shift left, bringing operational problems to the developers for handling, and a continuous focus on improvements.

Continuity also exists within marketing, HR and sales, and product development in insurance, manufacturing, pharmaceuticals, retail, transportation industries, and more. Continuity in these teams is handled with Scrum, Kanban, scale, or other agile methods.

But all agile methods share the commonality that they belong in the continuous lifespan, which is probably why agile teams also fit well with running continuous operations.

The four management methodologies from a lifespan perspective can be represented in the following table:

Management frameworks	Lifespan
Projects + Agile Projects	One time
Operation + Agile	Continuous

Experience

A successful project prerequisite is that the project can be accurately assessed before starting the implementation. This is the basis for the initial cost and budgeting, time plan, and quality metrics governing parts of the project contract. Projects require enough technical insight into the product delivery to break down the product into pieces that the organization can reliably estimate in order and effort. Changes will likely occur when executing the plan, so having previous knowledge of handling change is an example of processes that must be known in advance. There is bound to be a challenge in projects that can't be foreseen but knowing how to handle challenges and the magnitude of such challenges and whether they can be contained in the budget and plan or require a change decision are also prerequisites for successful projects. Successful projects require an organization that is working with known challenges.

Operation is known processes that are repetitive and similar in complexity. The most optimal process is doing precisely the same task because the process can be optimized to reduce waste by looking at triggers of the process and material used to optimize the specific process fully. Luckily the world is not so straightforward that everything can be put into fully optimized processes. When one process is optimized, it will affect another, and there's a constant need for managing processes to get value delivered with the least cost. This is what makes working with Lean optimization so enjoyable, as well as being the worker in the process that constantly oversees kaizen and performs mistake-proofing.

The idea in agile projects and agile development is that the details will be worked out as we go. It's iterative, learning and setting new goals for each iteration, not knowing the challenges we will face, and a high likelihood that the customers don't know what they want or what will work best. The agile method is relevant when there's high complexity or uncertainty. And when uncertainty is accepted in the delivery process. We don't want a customer expecting a product delivery in a fixed time, cost, or quality if the organization hasn't had any experience in a very similar delivery. Suppose an agreement on time, cost, or quality is needed. In that case, the agile project method might be relevant, but that has more to do if the delivery is a continuous effort or have a defined ending; it is not changing the uncertainty of the delivery teams' past experiences with similar deliveries. Agile is elegantly able to handle product development with unknown challenges.

The four management methodologies from an experience perspective can be represented in the following table:

Management frameworks	Experience
Projects + operation	Known Challenges
Agile Projects + Agile	Unknown Challenges

The quadrant

The two lifespan and experience perspectives can be represented as vertical and horizontal axes dividing a plane into quadrants. Each of the four management areas fills a quadrant to become a quadrant for understanding when to use which management framework: **P**rojects, **A**gile **P**rojects, **A**gile, and **O**peration.

This forms P-AP-A-O's idea to easily remember the order and the thoughts behind selecting the proper framework for the area to be managed.

Remembering the order by the name PAPAO resonates which management areas are one time or are continuous; and which management areas require previous experience or can solve unknown challenges.

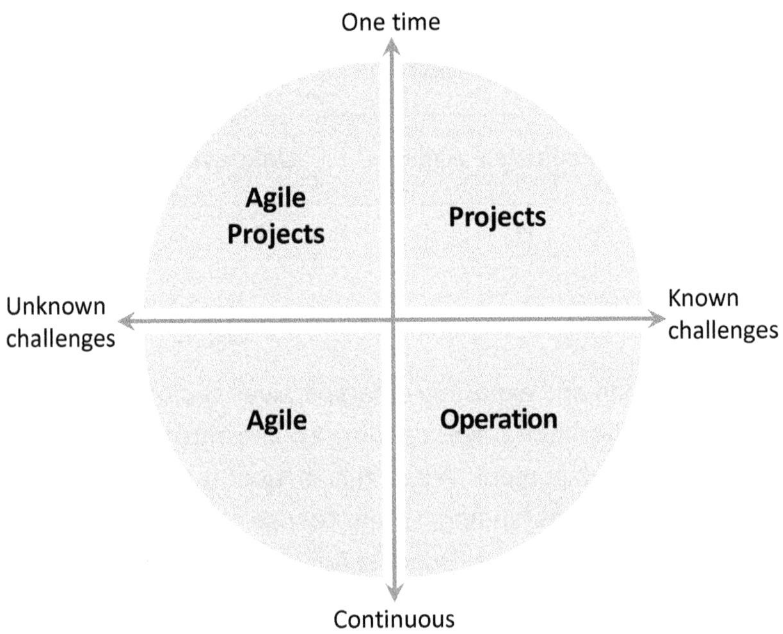

When put into practice, it can be difficult to determine or measure if the organizations' experience is enough to fall into the quadrants of known challenges.

Interoperability of the areas will help explain why it is relevant for organizations to master several areas simultaneously.

Interoperability

Agile projects

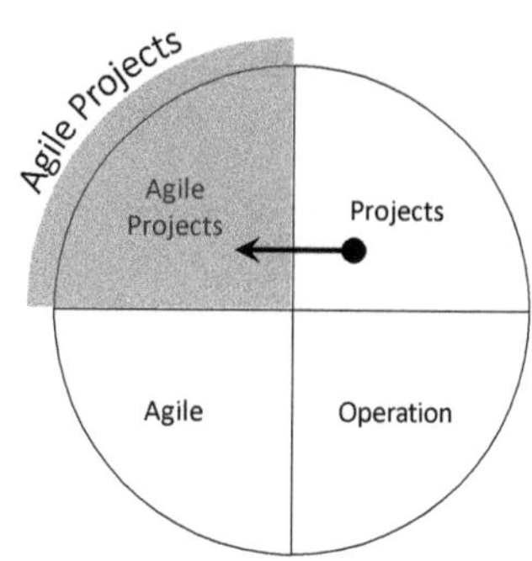

Information Technology initiatives like software development, platform transition, insourcing, and outsourcing are, as we have discussed, traditionally seen as Projects.

However, there is not enough experience in many projects to fall in the quadrant of "known challenge". While the project methodology can mitigate problems, it becomes dramatic when the project has to change when unknown challenges occur.

Letting the organization understand and accept that we don't have the experience or knowledge to breakdown the product structure nor estimate the effort or plan the execution alleviates the frustration of trying to plan the unknown.

We allow the execution to include investigating and likely even building before the final solution is understood.

This means that the solution that can be built is likely not what was perceived when the project started. Instead, it's a minimal viable product or a more straightforward solution that solves most of the business need.

An agile, iterative, problem-solving approach while driving towards ending and handing over the solution should be chosen, which we find in the agile project management area.

Projects in Agile

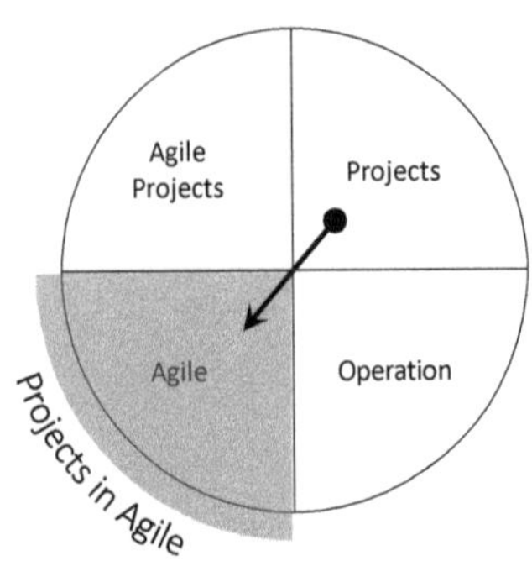

In Agile development, many projects can be solved, but agile can't handle all types of projects, so beware of the pitfalls.

There's no reason to consider the experience scale as a framework for solving unknown challenges benefits from previous experience.

The difference between projects and agile is the lifetime of projects; they are supposed to be ending and delivered to a customer.

Agile organizations can deliver these initiatives as it doesn't change from their usual process of incrementally delivering value. The pitfall is not to break the stable teams solving a project, instead let the agile organization handle it using agile methods.

SAFe uses Epics to collaborate on substantial deliveries across the organization. Like projects, SAFe deliveries can be measured against budget, quality, and time. Epics in SAFe also entail that the solution is likely to affect customers, so communication and release strategies must be considered. But make sure to transform the organization into scaled agile roles and responsibilities to handle large initiatives.

While agile can solve some projects, agile can't solve projects like building a bridge; Use traditional project management when it is obviously the best framework.

Agile transformation

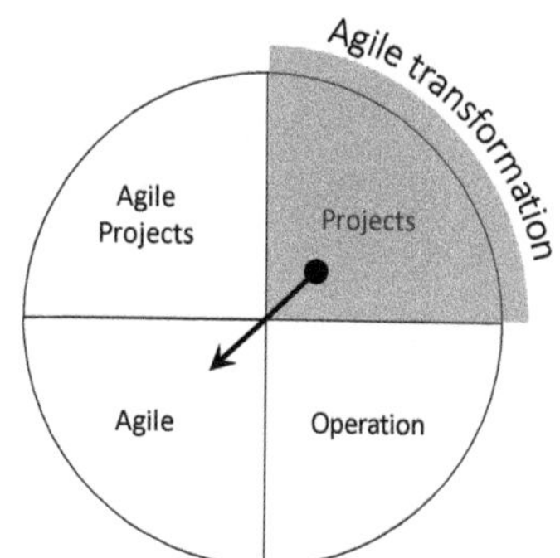

If the initiative is to transform an organization to agile methodology, it is a well-known organizational challenge (assuming you bring in experienced agile transformation leads).

These days agile transformation is in high demand, and there's plenty of highly experienced people able to help guide the organization towards a successful transformation. An agile project is not considered because it's challenging to transform into something using the same methods to transform; An agile project would only be relevant if the transformation were an unknown challenge.

And since you only need to transform the organization once into agile, it should be perceived as an organizational change project.

When the project is ended, the project is not handed over to operations as most projects are, but rather the organization is managed in the Agile quadrant from this day forth.

Develop operational processes

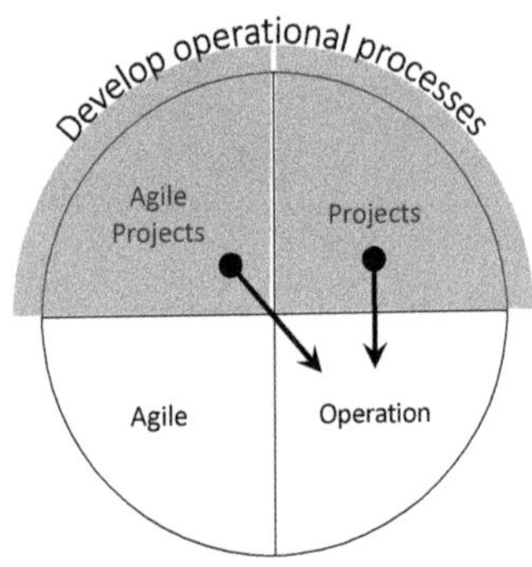

If the initiative is to set up operation processes, the project must be a one-time effort to transform the operational organization.

The organization does not have the knowledge nor the experience to build and implement new frameworks as part of their everyday work. They need experience from outside their department to create the best development and implementation approach.

They also need training in new ways of working like Lean, ITIL, and Six Sigma training, depending on the organizational transformation's quality requirement. There are two ways this can be accomplished with our management methods in a controlled and guided path for success: As a project or as an agile project. Both require a one-time effort to implement.

A project will rely on previous experience that knows the challenges and can guide the organization successfully towards the goal. Whereas an agile project, members of the operational organization are developing processes incrementally and learning as they go along.

This becomes a continuous improvement process that can be handled as an integral part of the operational management area.

DevOps

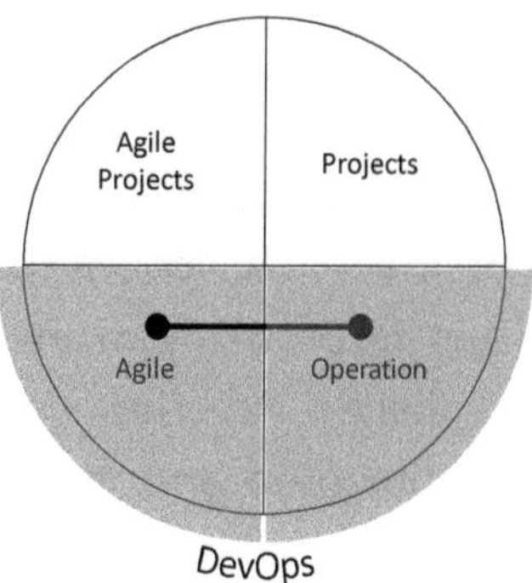

DevOps is interoperability between Agile and Operation. It is built into both of these rather than a framework for itself. DevOps cannot exist without agile nor operations.

DevOps entail that developers operate and operators are agile teams. The management practices of both agile and operation should be considered for optimal and effective DevOps.

Lean principles should always be an integral part of agile organizations. IT operation teams can enable development teams to monitor their solution and react to events rather than have support teams to do so.

It requires a mature software development organization before DevOps becomes effective; however, start and let DevOps mindset grow into the organization, or it could end up becoming a mountain to climb to start the journey towards effective DevOps.

Pitfalls

Beware of pitfalls when using the PAPAO management model. Organizations tend to need more experience to fall in the category of known challenges than you would think. Start with a mindset that it's probably an unknown challenge until proven to be a known challenge to the organization. Experience should be well documented and integrated into the organization before it is classified as known.

Another pitfall is scraping the old well-known methods to move towards a new management framework. Learn the new, but don't throw away the old and familiar. Beware of the old saying that everything looks like a nail if you only have a hammer. This is true in organizations and projects as well. Remember that the organization has a lot of experience, so instead, teach organizations to use the proper framework for the proper work type.

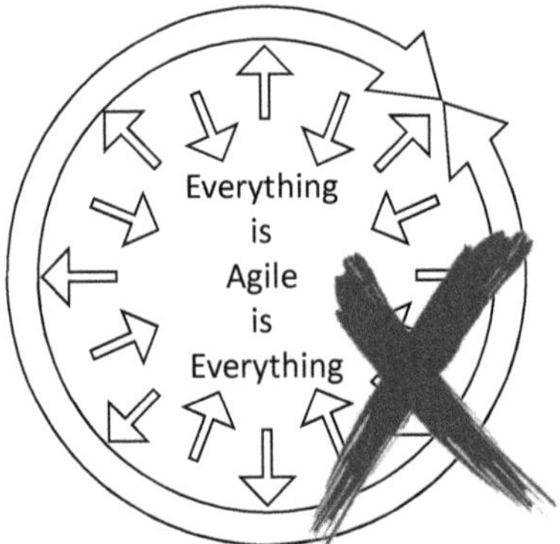

Interoperability of the PAPAO management model is crucial to effectiveness. And remember that the PAPAO management model only looks at the lifespan and experience of large initiatives; it's not a new strategy, governance, cost-benefit, architectural, or anything else model.

Fit for Frameworks

The following should not be taken as fact but as inspiration and to get you to start pondering what frameworks fit what purposes. Some frameworks overlap the PAPAO quadrants and thereby also each other. Make up your mind and discuss with your colleagues how your known implemented frameworks fit the PAPAO quadrants and what you can use from having multiple frameworks available for future initiatives.

PRINCE2

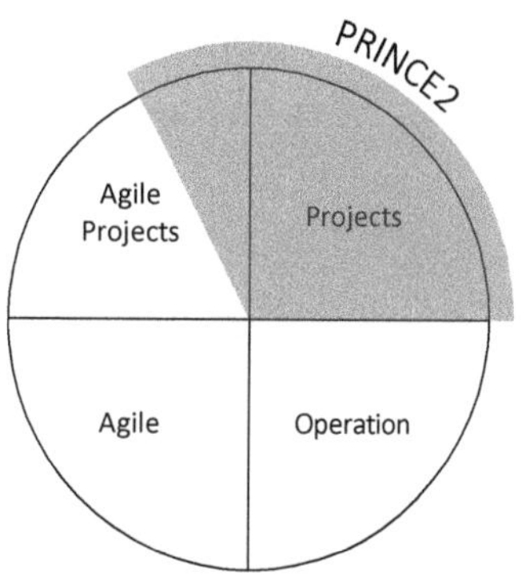

PRINCE2 methods are very closely connected to traditional project management. PRINCE2 is a stage-gate model with clear handover between stages that provides a controlled environment for deliveries that require adherence to requirements. This is well-aligned with delivery in controlled environments and following known processes. There's a close connection between the framework and the management area for which it is suitable. It is not a framework for delivering an unknown challenge or a continuous development. When having a fixed scope and fixed requirements, projects benefit from traditional project management methods.

PMBOK and PRINCE2 Agile

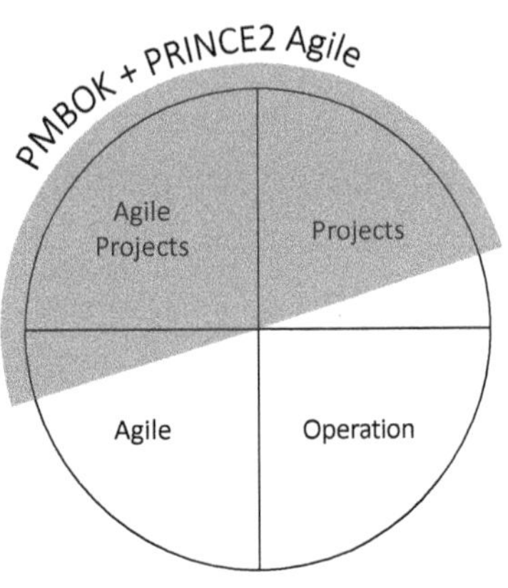

PMBOK and PRINCE2 Agile are hybrid and use relevant concepts from traditional projects and agile development. In a project-oriented organization, a continuous development can benefit from being solved using agile project management. Likewise, most traditional projects will benefit from being solved using agile project management.

Scrum

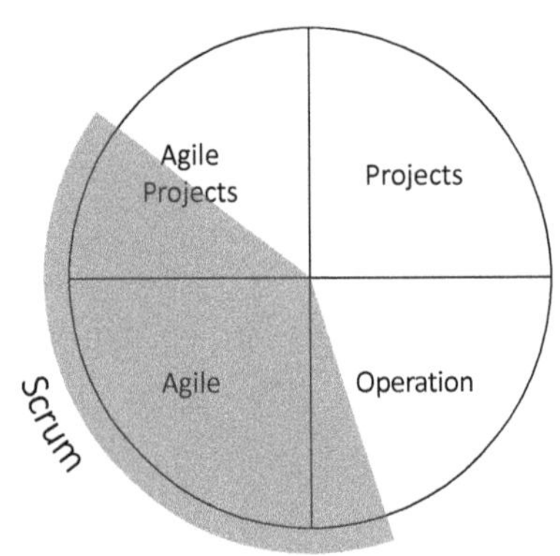

Scrum is the classic agile implementation that iteratively delivers products in the unknown space. Scrum is a method used in agile projects, but it's a lightweight framework that doesn't have the control mechanisms from scaled agile frameworks. While Scrum is used to deliver in agile projects, it can't solve every agile project as it is not an agile project management framework. In the operations space, Scrum provides a framework for some operational teams.

Read more about Scrum in the below book by Jakobsen, T. (2019) *Scrum Done Right*

ITIL, Lean, and Six Sigma

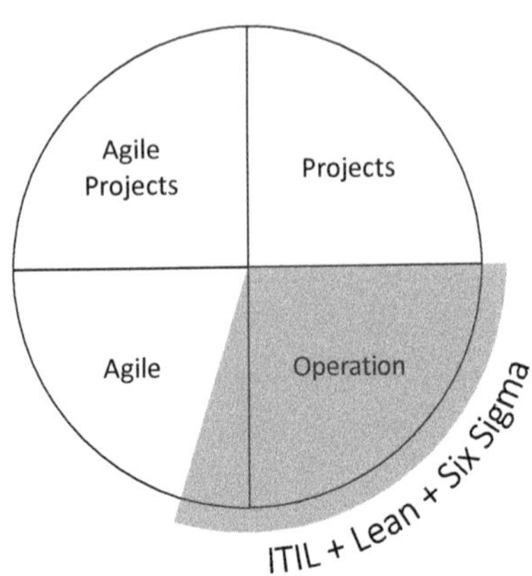

ITIL, Lean, and Six Sigma frameworks are the natural-born solutions for operations. Not only born in operations but a swiss army knife of how to optimize operations.

But the frameworks do more than that. Concepts from the world of Lean and Six Sigma are implemented in agile frameworks like Scaled Agile Framework (SAFe).

There's an interoperability need between agile and operation. That means that some continuous agile development can be solved using operational frameworks; however, only a fraction of the agile development could run as purely lean processes.

Scaled Agile Frameworks

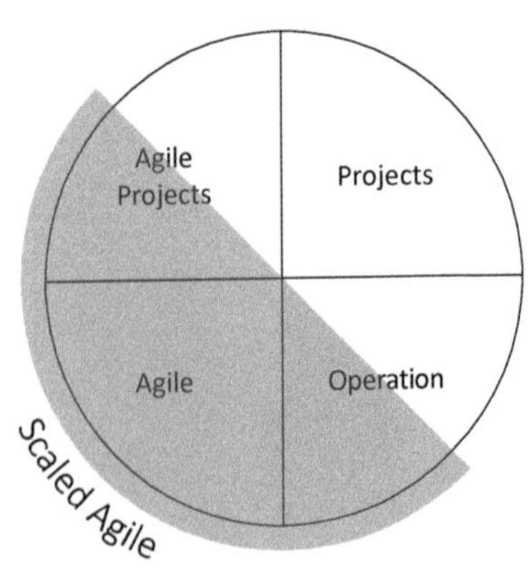

Scaled Agile Frameworks is a managed agile setup for large organizations that entails the entire organizational system and suggests an agile approach from strategic themes to individual team members.

More importantly, in this context, it can manage Epics equivalent to some agile projects and manage some operational tasks by implementing DevOps and operation in agile teams.

Kanban

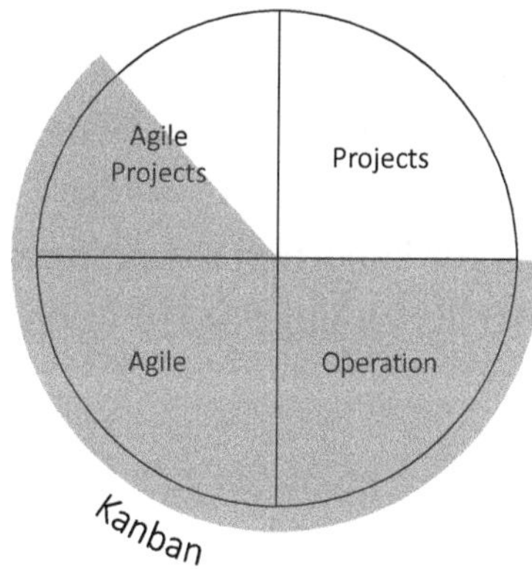

From the world of Lean Operation comes Kanban. It is foremost a visual system that shows progress and state of different tasks and can show bottlenecks and optimize throughput in the process. So generic that it is used in many other areas besides operation, even within classic project management.

Kanban method might fill up all model areas as Kanban has a universal application. However, that doesn't mean that Kanban can solve the entire quadrant of neither operation nor agile. Still, Kanban method spans from all of the operations area to a large part of the agile projects area, and perhaps more.

Let us at least agree that within operation and agile, including agile projects, Kanban is integrated and used repeatedly.

Conclusion

PAPAO is not a new framework or methodology; it's a model for perceiving the existing framework's applicability in modern management by looking at what differentiates these frameworks. But not least to explain the value that is still important to take from each management area, trying to avoid that organizations force one framework for all initiatives.

The team behind PAPAO hopes you will find it helpful in your future initiatives. We hope you will participate in the discussion on our web page with your insights, questions, and answers to other PAPAO Management Model readers.

Sincerely,

CaSandra Minichiello,
Agile Leader and
Transformational Coach

Dale Ray Thiesen,
Lean Philosophy Practitioner

Troels Jakobsen,
Lean Agile Coach and Trainer

Kasper Dannefer,
Lean Agile Coach and
Transformation Consultant

Thanks to Jim for input on
Project management frameworks.

www.ingramcontent.com/pod-product-compliance
Ingram Content Group UK Ltd.
Pitfield, Milton Keynes, MK11 3LW, UK
UKHW021924190726
13853UKWH00002B/831

9 788793 876309